W9-BTF-095

THE
EVOLUTION
OF YOU AND ME

MICHAEL BRIGHT

PowerKiDS
press™

Published in 2018 by **The Rosen Publishing Group, Inc.**
29 East 21st Street, New York, NY 10010

Cataloging-in-Publication Data
Names: Bright, Michael.
Title: The evolution of you and me / Michael Bright.
Description: New York : PowerKids Press, 2018. | Series: Planet Earth | Includes index.
Identifiers: ISBN 9781508153986 (pbk.) | ISBN 9781508153924 (library bound) | ISBN 9781508153818 (6 pack)
Subjects: LCSH: Evolution (Biology)--Juvenile literature. | Evolution--Juvenile literature.
Classification: LCC QH367.1 B69 2018 | DDC 576.8--dc23

Copyright © 2018 Wayland, a division of Hachette Children's Group

Written by Michael Bright
Cover illustration by Mark Turner
Editor: Corinne Lucas
Design: Grant Kempster and Alyssa Peacock

Picture credits: P 4 (t) © Stocktrek Images, Inc. / Alamy Stock Photo; P 4 (b) © gallimaufry/Shutterstock; P 5 (t) © Sisyphos23/ Wikimedia; P 5 (b) © CHRISTIAN DARKIN/SCIENCE PHOTO LIBRARY; P 6 © Michael Rosskothen/Shutterstock; P 7 (t) © DEAGOSTINI/UIG/SCIENCE PHOTO LIBRARY; P 7 (b) © JAIME CHIRINOS/SCIENCE PHOTO LIBRARY; P 8 (t) © Andreas Meyer/ Shutterstock; P 8 (b) © Martin Shields / Alamy Stock Photo; P 9 (t) © B. O'Kane / Alamy Stock Photo; P 9 (b) © Matt9122/ Shutterstock; P 10 (t) © Mauricio Anton; P 10 (b) © reptiles4all/Shutterstock; P 11 (t) © dpa picture alliance archive / Alamy Stock Photo; P 11 (b) © Catmando/Shutterstock; P 12 (t) © The Natural History Museum / Alamy Stock Photo; P 12 (b) © SanderMeertinsPhotography/Shutterstock; P 13 (t) © Discott/Wikimedia; P 13 (b) © Roger Hall/SCIENCE PHOTO LIBRARY; P 14 © Herschel Hoffmeyer/Shutterstock; P 15 (t) © Daderot/Wikimedia; P 15 (b) © MarcelClemens/Shutterstock; P 16 © B Christopher / Alamy Stock Photo; P 17 (t) © RAUL MARTIN/MSF/SCIENCE PHOTO LIBRARY; P 17 (b) © The Art Archive / Alamy Stock Photo; P 18 (t) © P.PLAILLY/E.DAYNES/SCIENCE PHOTO LIBRARY; P 18 (b) © MAURICIO ANTON/SCIENCE PHOTO LIBRARY; P 19 (t) © B Christopher / Alamy Stock Photo; P 21 (t) © Elenarts/Shutterstock; P 21 (m) © Creativemarc/Shutterstock; P 21 (b) © NordNordWest/Wikimedia; P 22 © Cro Magnon / Alamy Stock Photo; P 23 (t) © Asia Photopress / Alamy Stock Photo; P 23 (b) © B Christopher / Alamy Stock Photo; P 24 (r) © KENNIS AND KENNIS/MSF/SCIENCE PHOTO LIBRARY; P 25 © Creativemarc/ Shutterstock; P 26 © blickwinkel / Alamy Stock Photo; P 27 © Universal Images Group North America LLC / DeAgostini / Alamy Stock Photo; P 28 (t) © Valentyna Chukhlyebova/Shutterstock; P 28 (b) © Stocktrek Images, Inc. / Alamy Stock Photo; P 29 (t) © GARY HINCKS/SCIENCE PHOTO LIBRARY; P 29 (b) © Wollertz/Shutterstock.

Manufactured in China
CPSIA Compliance Information: Batch #BS17PK: For Further Information contact Rosen Publishing, New York, New York at 1-800-237-9932.

contents

time of
OPPORTUNITY

The Cenozoic **era** started about 66 million years ago (mya) and its name means "new life." With the dinosaurs and three-quarters of the world's plants and animals killed in a **mass extinction**, it marked the end of the Age of Reptiles and the start of the next chapter in the story of Planet Earth — the Age of Mammals. Among the survivors were the primates, the group of mammals that includes us, humans. This is the story of you, me, and our earliest **ancestors** who lived in the trees.

up in the trees

The very first primate-like animals lived at the same time as the dinosaurs of the mid-Cretaceous period, about 85 mya. Many primates survived the mass extinction that wiped out the dinosaurs, and one of the survivors was the rat-sized *Purgatorius*. This was a special primate. Its main feature was an anklebone that gave it flexible feet similar to those of modern tree-climbing primates. It means our ancestors were **agile** tree-dwellers, who probably fed on insects and fruit, and were similar in shape to modern tree shrews.

Mammals have fur or hair.

Night-active tarsiers have big eyes.

first features

By 56 mya, 10 million years after the dinosaurs became extinct, primates were beginning to show features that we recognize in ourselves today. *Teilhardina*, for example, was a tarsier-like primate that had flat nails on its fingers and toes, rather than claws. Our earliest ancestors had nails like us.

Geological Timeline

Era	Period	Epoch
Cenozoic (66 mya to present)	Quaternary (2.588 mya to present)	Holocene (11,700 years to present)
		Pleistocene 2.58 mya to 11,700 years)
	Neogene (23.03 mya to 2.58 mya)	Pliocene (5.333 mya to 2.58 mya)
		Miocene (23.03 mya to 5.333 mya)
	Paleogene (66 mya to 23.03 mya)	Oligocene (33.9 mya to 23.03 mya)
		Eocene (56 mya to 33.9 mya)
		Paleocene (66 mya to 56 mya)

on the ground

With the dinosaurs gone, **carnivorous** mammals called mesonychians took over as top **predators**, but they came from an unexpected family. They were distantly related to pigs and have been described as "wolves with hooves," although one **species**, *Ankalagon,* was the size of a bear.

WORKING TOGETHER

Early primate-like mammals, such as *Carpolestes*, ate fruit. Their eyes did not face forwards like modern primates. This **evolved** later, and it is possible that primates and fruiting trees evolved together. The trees produced something attractive to primates — fruit — and the primates ate the fruit and spread its seeds. The fruit became increasingly more attractive and the primates developed forward-pointing eyes to find it and hands to grasp it. This is called co-evolution.

Carpolestes had toenails but claws on its fingers.

Andrewsarchus was related to hippos.

THE BIRDS
are coming!

The mammals were not the only group to develop into dangerous predators after the dinosaurs disappeared. Perhaps surprisingly, the birds did too, and they were monsters! Birds were the top predators in South America for over 50 million years. It was as if the giant dinosaurs were living again, which, in a way they were — birds are living dinosaurs! These giants were the terror birds.

killer birds

Kelenken was a terror bird that stood 10 feet (3 m) tall. It had the biggest bird skull that has ever been found, with a large, 18-inch (46 cm) long beak, similar to an eagle's. It was flightless but a fast runner, reaching speeds of about 30 miles per hour (48 kph). This terrifying predator ran down smaller animals, which it killed by first kicking them with its feet to injure them. Then the bird would hold them tight with its enormous hooked **talons** and rip off the flesh with its hooked beak.

BIG SQUEEZE

With the competition from dinosaurs gone, other reptiles grew to monster sizes. Titanoboa was a giant snake that looked like a boa constrictor and behaved like an anaconda. It probably spent most of its life in the water. It was up to 42 feet (12.8 m) long and weighed more than 2,200 pounds (1 metric ton), making it the longest and heaviest snake ever discovered. It lived in South American swamps, where it hunted giant freshwater turtles twice the size of garbage can lids and lungfish longer than a person.

Another flightless giant was *Gastornis*. It grew up to 6.6 feet (2 m) tall and was similar in shape to the terror birds. The difference was that it lacked a hook on its beak and its feet did not have large claws. *Gastornis* had a powerful bite, but it is more likely to have been a plant eater, rather than a predator, probably feeding on tough plant material and hard seeds, like a parrot.

Its jaws could expand to swallow large prey.

hot and cold EARTH

Most of the Paleocene **epoch** had been cool, but towards the end, and during the following Eocene epoch, 56–34 mya, the world became considerably warmer. There was little ice anywhere on Earth and forests covered large parts of the planet from pole to pole. It was a paradise for small primates.

The first wing finger has a claw.

dawn monkey

While the birds were increasing in size and **ferocity** on the ground, our primate ancestors were small and hiding away in the trees. *Eosimius*, meaning "dawn monkey," lived about 45 mya. While not the direct ancestor of monkeys, apes, and us, it was probably closely related. It was small enough to fit into the palm of your hand and was shaped like a tiny modern tarsier (see page 4). It ate insects and nectar, and was most likely **nocturnal**.

first known bat

The oldest known flying mammals appeared at this time. It was the fourth time animals had taken to the air. After insects, reptiles, and birds had all flown, it was the turn of the bats. *Icaronycteris* was an early bat with a wingspan of 15 inches (37 cm), and was capable of powered flight.

early marine mammals

The largest animal in Eocene epoch seas was *Basilosaurus*, a **primitive** type of whale. It was eel-shaped, up to 66 feet (20 m) long, and had enormous tooth-filled jaws. Its front legs were like small paddles and its back legs were tiny. It could not dive deep or swim like modern whales, but it had a crushing bite and fed on bony fish and sharks, such as the newly evolving tiger sharks.

Fossil backbone of *Basilosaurus*.

CLIMATE CHANGE

At the end of the Eocene epoch, everything changed again. A couple of large asteroids crashed into Siberia, Russia, and Chesapeake Bay. The dust blotted out the Sun and Earth's temperature dropped, causing ice to reappear at the North and South poles. Many species became extinct, including some of the new mammals that had evolved, but the primates survived again.

The early forms of tiger sharks appeared in Eocene seas.

ANCIENT
and modern

Scientists think of the Oligocene epoch (34–23 mya) as the changeover from early life-forms to more modern plants and animals. The climate was generally cooler and tropical forests that had previously covered much of the Earth were giving way to grasslands. Living on this more open landscape was the largest mammal the world has ever seen, but our ancestors were still up in the trees.

goodbye monkeys

Monkeys and apes parted ways on the human timeline 30–25 mya. Two fossil primates have been found that show this split. One led to monkeys, such as baboons, and the other to the apes and us. *Rukwapithecus* was the ape and *Nsungwepithecus* was the monkey. They both lived in Africa when it was colliding with Europe and Asia. The chaotic geological events might have led one group to find different food sources than the other, so they developed in different ways.

This modern-day ape evolved from *Rukwapithecus*.

Nsungwepithecus is the ancestor of baboons like this one.

first feline

The first cat, *Proailurus*, also appeared at this time. Resembling a modern genet shown in the image to the left, it was about the size of a domestic cat with large eyes, a long tail, sharp teeth and claws. It lived partly on the ground and partly in the trees … a real threat to our primate ancestors.

ocean gliders

Out at sea, the flying birds were giants. *Pelagornis* was the largest flying bird ever to be discovered. It had a wingspan of 24 feet (7.4 m), twice the size of a wandering albatross — the bird with the largest wingspan alive today. It probably soared over the ocean, kept in the air by wind currents rising up from ocean waves.

oversized rhinos

The largest known land mammal during the Oligocene epoch was *Paraceratherium*, a huge hornless rhinoceros. It was 25 feet (7.5 m) long, stood 16 feet (5 m) at the shoulder, and weighed up to 44,000 pounds (20 metric tons). This giant had few enemies, but huge 36-foot-long (11 m) crocodiles must have attacked it, judging from the bite marks found on fossils of leg bones.

Paraceratherium was one of the largest land mammals ever to exist.

11

planet of THE APES

The Miocene epoch, 23–5.3 mya, was the Age of the Apes. Scientists have identified at least 100 different types of apes living at the time, but which one led to us? Scientists are finding fossils that might give us some clues.

ape-monkey

A 3.3-foot-long (1 m) primate called *Proconsul* lived 25–23 mya. It was once thought to be the ancestor of all the apes, but it had both monkey-like and ape-like features. When traveling through the trees, it probably ran on all fours on the tops of branches, a feature of monkeys. But it had no tail and was better able to grasp things, which is ape-like. With this mix, *Proconsul* was probably not our direct ancestor.

Pliobates resembled a modern gibbon, like this lar gibbon.

mother of all apes

Most great apes today are large-bodied animals, so scientists used to believe that the ancestor of all the apes was a chunky animal, like *Proconsul*. They thought smaller fossils were of lesser apes, such as gibbons. Imagine their surprise when they discovered a primate they named *Pliobates* that lived 11.6 mya. It was small and had a face like a gibbon, but a big brain for its size. However, its most interesting features were its elbow and wrist bones. They could rotate to allow it to climb easily, a feature of the great apes and not the gibbons. This little guy could have been our early ape ancestor!

monster ape

About 9 mya, an ancient relative of the orangutan was a monster ape. It was called *Gigantopithecus*, and it was the largest ape that has ever lived. It stood 10 feet (3 m) tall, almost twice the height of an average adult human. Some people think it is still alive today and hiding in the Himalayas — the mythical yeti or abominable snowman.

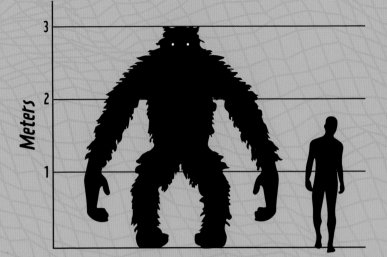

Gigantopithecus compared to a human

Cheek teeth could grind tough plant material, such as bamboo and seeds.

Gigantopithecus probably walked like a gorilla or chimpanzee.

13

a time for
WHALES

While the apes were developing on land, big things were happening at sea. During the Miocene and Pliocene epochs, 23–2.5 mya, the oceans were filling with mammals that had abandoned the land and returned to the sea — the whales, dolphins, seals, and sea lions. Lurking in wait for them were the predators, including giant sharks.

leviathan

This time could also be called the Age of Whales because many new species were swimming in the seas. One became a gigantic hunter. *Livyatan melvillei* was a giant sperm whale with the biggest bite of any known mammal or reptile. It was similar in length to a modern bull sperm whale.

Today's sperm whales have teeth only in the lower jaw, but *Livyatan* had enormous teeth in both jaws. The longest were 14 inches (36 cm), the longest teeth (aside from tusks) ever known. Scientists think it hunted other whales.

early seals

Other **marine** mammals appearing at this time were the seals, such as the 8-foot-long (2.4 m) *Allodesmus*. They evolved from predators shaped like modern otters and they hunted fish and squid, but they had to watch their backs. Hunting the hunters was a ferocious walrus named the *Pelagiarctos*. It was up to 10 feet (3 m) long, had a powerful bite and ate seals.

Allodesmus swam using its front flippers like a sea lion.

Livyatan probably ate other whales.

megalodon

Whale **blubber** is a high-energy food and, even today, the largest types of sharks relish it. One of the fiercest whale hunters of the Miocene and Pliocene epochs must have been *Carcharodon megalodon*, a gigantic version of a great white shark. At 59 feet (18 m) long, it was one of the largest ever ocean predators. Its jaws were lined with 6-inch (15 cm) **serrated** teeth, and fortunately for us, it died out 2.6 mya.

early
WALKERS

Back on the land, the next stage in the evolution of you and me was about 7 mya, when we split away from our nearest relatives, the chimpanzees. This marked the arrival of small human-like apes that stood upright. Scientists once thought that our ancestors came down from the trees to live on the **savanna**, and this is why they walked upright, but new discoveries reveal that they still spent much of the time in the trees, but walked upright on the ground.

ape-walking

Flat face with heavy **brow ridges** on the forehead.

In the Miocene epoch, two apes from Africa, both living at about the same time we separated from the chimpanzees, give a glimpse of what this stage in the ape-to-human story might have looked like. *Sahelanthropus* lived 7 mya, making it one of the oldest known species in the human family tree, and *Orrorin* lived 6 mya. They were both about the size of a chimpanzee, had small brains, and grasping hands for climbing. But they probably also walked upright when on the ground.

standing up

"Ardi" is the nickname for *Ardipithecus,* who lived about 5–4 mya. She was not like a chimpanzee and not like a human, but something in between. Her teeth suggest she was probably a general **omnivore**. She was 3.9 feet (1.2 m) tall, and was **bipedal**, which meant she walked upright. Ardi also climbed trees, and she lived in woodlands in what is now Ethiopia.

Bipedal on the ground but **quadrupedal** in the trees.

lucy

"Lucy" lived about 3.2 mya, also in Ethiopia. She was an australopithecine — pronounced "aw-strey-loh-pith-uh-seen." This means "southern ape-man," and Lucy was given the scientific name *Australopithecus afarensis*. She had an ape-like flat nose, jutting jaw, and a bigger brain than Ardi. She walked more like us than a chimpanzee, so she was also a better walker than Ardi. Males were bigger than females, about 4.9 feet (1.5 m) tall, a little taller than a chimpanzee. The species may have used pieces of sharp stones for cutting meat from bones, the earliest record of tool use.

Lucy's canine teeth were less pointed than in other apes.

SOUTHERN
ape-men and
RELATIVES

Lucy was one of several species of australopithecines living during the Pliocene epoch. They were all slender omnivores and lived in the same parts of Africa as bulky plant-eating ape-men. There was also at least one that resembled humans more than any of the others.

southern apes of africa

Australopithecus africanus lived at about the same time as Lucy, but in southern Africa. The species had a mix of human and ape features. It had a rounded skull, bigger brain, and smaller teeth than Lucy's species, but it still had the long arms of an ape and an ape-like face. Males were 4.5 feet (1.38 m) tall and females were slightly smaller. They walked upright but could also climb.

weird walking

One species, *Australopithecus sediba*, walked more than it climbed, but it walked in an unusual way. At each step it turned its foot inwards so its weight pushed down on the outside edge of the foot. Despite this strange way of walking, it had long arms and a small body, like other australopithecines.

nutcracker man

Paranthropus had a **sagittal crest** on the top of its head, like a male gorilla, and flaring cheekbones that anchored powerful jaw muscles, giving the animal a disc-shaped face. Nicknamed "nutcracker man," it had big cheek teeth, four times the size of ours, and they had the thickest covering of **enamel** of any known ape. They ground tough plant materials. *Paranthropus* was about the same height as *Australopithecus africanus* but much heavier, and lived in east and south Africa.

Paranthropus had a round face.

handy man

Living alongside the ape-men and nutcrackers in east Africa was a more human-like ape, the earliest known example of our group. It has been given the species name *Homo habilis*, meaning "handy man," because stone tools were found close to its fossilized skeleton. It had a slightly larger brain than the ape-men, but still had long ape-like arms. Scientists are unsure whether it is one of our direct ancestors, but it was probably close to the line that led to us.

Handy man made tools.

early HUMANS

In Africa, about 1.8 mya during the Pleistocene epoch, an early human, named *Homo erectus*, meaning "upright man," had a bigger brain than any of its **predecessors**. Scientists have linked this increase in brain size to the use of fire and more complex tools.

upright man

Homo erectus was the first early human to have human-like proportions to its body. Its legs were long and its arms were short. It did not look like an ape — it looked more like us. Some males stood 6.1 feet (1.85 m) tall. This was a creature more suited to life on the ground than in the trees. It could walk and run, and it probably looked after old, sick, and weak individuals.

Males were 25% larger than females.

cooking

The fires made by *Homo erectus* might have been used for cooking, although at present there is no definite evidence. Even so, cooked food would have been easier and quicker to digest, and provided the nutrients and energy needed for tall bodies with big brains.

Refined stone tools.

tools and fire

Homo erectus used tools — not simple tools made from stone **shards**, but more complex hand axes and cleavers, and probably made campfires. This would have kept predators away at night, and these early humans might have sat around the fire and maybe even talked together. This species probably formed the first **hunter-gatherer** societies. The group hunted together to get meat, gathered fruits, nuts, and seeds, collected honey, and dug up roots.

Skull found in Dmanisi, Georgia.

asian traveler

Most early humans lived in the southern half of Africa, but *Homo erectus* was one of the first early humans to move out of Africa. Fossil discoveries have been made in China and the Indonesian islands. It might even have been the first early human to use rafts to cross the sea. It is not known whether it found its way to Europe, but fossils have been found in nearby Georgia and stone tools of the right age in Turkey.

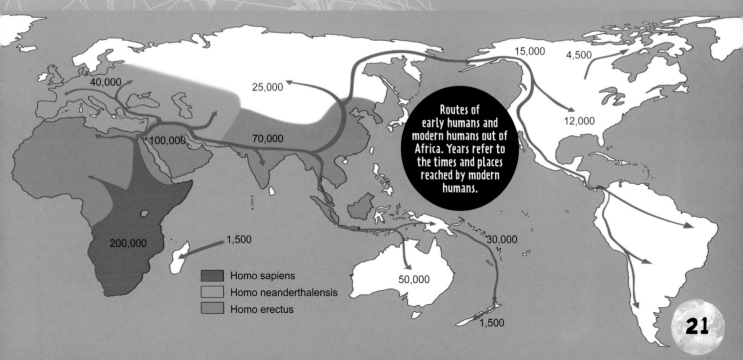

40,000

25,000

15,000   4,500

100,000   70,000

12,000

Routes of early humans and modern humans out of Africa. Years refer to the times and places reached by modern humans.

200,000   1,500

30,000

50,000

Homo sapiens
Homo neanderthalensis
Homo erectus

1,500

neanderthals and
HOBBITS

During the Pleistocene epoch 2.5 million to 11,700 years ago, several types of early human lived in various parts of the world, including the Neanderthals. One of the challenges they faced was the series of ice ages that saw vast ice sheets covering parts of the Earth.

heidelberg man

Homo heidelbergensis lived about 700,000 years ago. It was the first of our early relatives to **migrate** from tropical Africa to the colder parts of Europe. These pre-humans were up to 5.7 feet (1.8 m) tall and stocky, so their body had a smaller surface area to lose heat from than the upright, tropical-living *Homo erectus*. They were the first to build shelters of wood and rock, and they made wooden spears tipped with stone. They were also the first early humans known to hunt together to bring down large animals, such as mammoths.

Homo heidelbergensis's brain was almost as large as ours.

22

neanderthal man

Neanderthals were our closest extinct relatives. They **diverged** from Heidelberg man about 300,000 years ago. Their body was shorter and more thickset than modern humans, but their brain was larger than ours. They had a thick brow ridge above the eyes, and a large nose to warm cold, dry air. They were well adapted to survive in the colder conditions that accompanied the ice ages.

Large eye sockets mean better eyesight than ours.

Neanderthals had a barrel-shaped chest and short legs.

HOBBITS

The fossil remains of *Homo floresiensis* were discovered on the island of Flores, Indonesia. This pre-human was just over 3 feet (1 m) tall and had short legs and big feet, which is why it was given the nickname "Hobbit." It made stone tools, hunted pygmy elephants, and avoided giant Komodo dragons. It lived between 95,000 and 17,000 years ago, so it would have encountered modern people.

the first florists

Neanderthals controlled fire, lived in shelters, made and wore clothes, hunted large animals, gathered plant foods, and even created ornaments. They deliberately buried their dead and marked the occasion with flowers. No other early humans had done such a thing.

23

modern
HUMANS

Our species *Homo sapiens* branched off from *Homo heidelbergensis* about 200,000 years ago in Africa; but not all of those humans stayed on the continent for long. A handful left and went on to populate the world.

complex brain

Homo sapiens means "wise person." We have a large and complicated brain, so we are good at solving problems. We appreciate the past and anticipate something happening in the future. We have language and live in complex societies. We are intensely **inquisitive**, with the desire to learn and create, which is why we have developed the science and art we have today.

Large brains led to complex languages.

ultimate tool user

Our species stands upright and we walk on two legs. We show skillful use of our hands and we make and use the most complex tools of any known species. We are the only animals living today that build fires and cook food.

out of africa

At some point between 125,000 and 60,000 years ago, humans moved out of Africa (see page 21). Only a few hundred are thought to have been in the **vanguard**, probably migrating during warm, wet spells between ice ages. The travelers reached as far east as Australia by about 50,000 years ago. During their journeys, they came across other early human species, such as the Neanderthals in Europe. Shortly after these encounters, the more primitive groups died out. Our role in their disappearance is unclear.

HOMO SAPIENS

One of the first early humans in Europe.

HOMO ANTECESSOR

Interbred with humans.

HOMO NEANDERTHALENSIS

HOMO ERECTUS

ICE AGES

While *Homo sapiens* were evolving, parts of the planet became very cold. It was the time of the ice ages, when ice sheets covered Europe, North America and Siberia. There was not just one but several, each cold phase interrupted by short periods of warm and wet conditions. Human evolution was influenced greatly by the dramatic climate changes. It may have caused us to be more intelligent and adaptable. *Homo sapiens* had to be clever to survive.

kingdom of
THE HORSE

Separate to our own development, scientists have a fairly complete history about the horse in North America. The story started with a dog-sized creature of the rainforest and ended with the fleet-footed runner on the open plains that people tamed.

first horse

Eohippus was one of the first horses to appear about 52 mya. It was the size of a fox and scampered about in its rainforest home. It had spread-out toes that did not sink into the soft forest floor, but its legs were quite long. It **browsed** on low, soft foliage and fruits.

middle horse

About 40 mya, a drier climate meant that forests were giving way to grasslands, and the next horse-like mammal was better adapted to live in more open **habitats**. *Mesohippus* was 24 inches (60 cm) tall at the shoulder, had long legs for running fast, and teeth capable of grinding tougher plant material.

Fossil skeleton of *Eohippus.*

wild horse herds

By 30 mya, *Merychippus* stood about 3.3 feet (1 m) tall, had a long horse-like **muzzle**, and eyes wide apart so it could watch all around for predators. It lived in herds and was the first horse to **graze** grass rather than browse on bushes.

evolution to true horses

About 3.5 mya, the oldest known true horse evolved. *Equus simplicidens* was up to 5 feet (1.5 m) tall at the shoulder, stocky like a Grevy's zebra, but had a donkey-like head. It gave rise to the modern horse.

Mesohippus

Merychippus

going, going, gone

Horses expanded their **range** and migrated one of two ways. Some left North America for Asia via a temporary land bridge (see page 28), eventually ending up in Europe. Others headed south during the ice ages, but by 10,000 years ago, they were extinct, along with other large mammals that were living in North America at the same time.

the humans ARE COMING!

During the peak of each ice age, the sea level was lower than it is today. It exposed a strip of land between Alaska and Siberia that had previously been under the sea. Many animals migrated across this land bridge, some going one way and some the other. Among the travelers to North America were parties of human hunters. They became the first Native Americans.

north american mammals

Large mammals, such as mammoths and mastodons, lived in North America at the time humans arrived. There were also horses, giant beavers, tapirs, pig-like peccaries, antelope-like saiga, and camels. Predators included short-faced bears, American lions and cheetahs, dire wolves, scimitar-toothed cats, and the stocky and ferocious saber-toothed cat *Smilodon*.

all change!

Three mya, the lands of North and South America also began to join together. At first, animals hopped from one island to the next, but then a land bridge allowed the northern species to head south and southern species to go north. It was called the Great American Interchange. Heading north were giant ground sloths, capybara and the giant armadillo-like *Glyptotherium*.

Red arrows show the flow of human migration across the Bering land bridge.

THE BERING LAND BRIDGE

Grizzly bears survived the mass extinction.

extinction

Then, between 11,500 and 10,000 years ago many of these large mammals and their predators suddenly disappeared. The survivors were bison, moose, gray wolves, caribou, grizzly and black bears, musk ox, and mountain sheep and goats, all from Asia. The native American animals had not encountered people before, but the Asian species had lived alongside them. Did the migrant animals instinctively know the danger from human hunters, even though they had been separated from them for thousands of years?

who done it?

The extinction of the large mammals in North America is puzzling to scientists and raises questions. It happened at the end of the last ice age, so was it the result of a major climate change? Or, did those human migrants from Asia kill them all? It is hard to ignore the coincidence of both of these situations, but nobody really knows the answer.

glossary

agile able to move quickly and easily

ancestor animal from which later animals evolved

bipedal walking on two legs

blubber fatty tissue under the skin that keeps a whale warm

brow ridge ridge of bone on the forehead, above the eyes

browse eat from bushes and low trees

carnivorous meat-eating

diverge develop in a different direction

enamel hard white material covering teeth

epoch geological time span between "period" and "age"

era geological time span between "eon" and "period"

evolve develop gradually

ferocity extreme aggressiveness

graze eat grasses

habitat particular type of place where an animal lives

hunter-gatherer one who hunts animals and collects plant material

inquisitive very interested in something

marine to do with the sea

mass extinction disappearance of many plants and animals at the same time

migrate move from one place to another

muzzle part of the head that sticks out in front, including nose, mouth, and jaws — also known as a snout

nocturnal active at night

omnivore eats both plants and animals

predator animal that hunts and eats other animals

predecessor one that comes before

primitive early stage of development

quadrupedal walking on four legs

range area in which an animal or plant lives or grows

sagittal crest ridge of bone running along the top of the skull

savanna tropical grasslands

serrated jagged like a saw blade

shard piece of rock with sharp edges

society community of animals

species type of plant or animal

talons large claws on a predator's feet

vanguard out in front

Books

Evolution Revolution (2016)
Robert Winston
DK Children

Evolution: The Whole Life on Earth Story (2014)
Glenn Murphy
Pan Macmillan

Evolution: Why Did Fish Grow Feet? And Other Stories of Life on Earth (2014)
Anne Rooney
Ticktock Books

Totally Human (2011)
Cynthia Pratt Nicolson
Kids Can Press

Websites

PowerKids Press has developed an online list of websites related to the subject of this book. This site is updated regularly. Please use this link to access the list:
www.powerkidslinks.com/pe/evolution

index